SIXTIES SPOTTING DAYS
AROUND THE
SOUTHERN REGION

SIXTIES SPOTTING DAYS AROUND THE SOUTHERN REGION

Kevin Derrick

AMBERLEY

This edition first published 2016

Amberley Publishing
The Hill, Stroud
Gloucestershire, GL5 4EP

www.amberley-books.com

Copyright © Kevin Derrick, 2016

The right of Kevin Derrick to be identified as
the Author of this work has been asserted in
accordance with the Copyrights, Designs and
Patents Act 1988.

ISBN 978 1 4456 6083 7 (print)
ISBN 978 1 4456 6084 4 (ebook)

British Library Cataloguing in Publication Data.
A catalogue record for this book is available from
the British Library.

Typesetting by Amberley Publishing.
Printed in the UK.

Contents

Spotters of the time take note at Waterloo as No. 34064 *Fighter Command* runs out for Nine Elms light engine in 1962. (Trans Pennine Publishing)

Introduction

To some enthusiasts the Southern Region lacks appeal, when it is seen through eyes that had little interest for the many types of electric multiple units that prevailed during the sixties. However to those of us who grew up within the region's boundaries, perhaps fondness for both the EMUs, 'Spam Cans' or the possibly ugly Bulleid Qrs was inevitable.

Although the Southern Railway had enjoyed government assistance with finance during the Depression of the 1930s to complete the Brighton electrification, the onset of the Second World War generally put the brakes firmly on any further schemes until the early sixties, when development across Kent and the extension of the third rail to Bournemouth began.

Fortunes had been spent to rebuild all of the Merchant Navy Pacifics and many of the Light Pacifics as well. However the orders for diesels and electric locomotives still went ahead, even though it was envisaged that units would be used on all but the Weymouth and Southampton boat trains. Even the Isle of Wight would not be spared the progress of EMUs, even if they would be very second-hand thirty-year-old London Transport tube stock. How much better if the Isle of Wight had been like the Isle of Man, then we would have a steam network to attract tourists and day trippers today.

For anyone born in the mid to late 1950s in perhaps the north of Scotland, Devon, Cornwall or East Anglia, then their memories of steam would be thin on the ground as everything would have been dieselised or vanished before their experiences or memories had set in their childhood. For your author as a child of the late fifties and early sixties I was fortunate to be within earshot of Feltham marshalling yards and shed, and just a pocket-money ride away in a rake of 4-SUBs to perhaps Clapham Junction or Waterloo. Such expeditions would be with the regulation duffle bag, a grown up's Thermos flask, rounds of soggy cheese and tomato sandwiches and if lucky a Mars Bar. Joining the many others with similar interest on the platforms often led to joining groups on shed bashes, official or not, and before long adventures countrywide funded by modest wages from paper rounds. Does this sound familiar to you as a reader as well?

If like us you enjoy a little bit of nostalgia join us in a good wallow again back in time within both the Sixties and Seventies Spotting Days series.

Kevin Derrick
Boat of Garten

Waterloo to
Clapham
Junction

How many of us have spent a great number of hours sat on Post Office trolleys or the BRUTE type that began replacing them in the sixties. Many Standard 4MTs came to the Southern Region second-hand, but this example, No. 80015, spent all its working life around the Southern's metals. Engaged such as on this day in empty stock duties at Waterloo in October 1966. (Strathwood Library Collection)

Both firemen have their U Class Moguls Nos 31791 and 31639 up to the mark as they await departure from Waterloo for the first leg of the RCTS Longmoor Flyer as far as Woking on 30 April 1966. (Aldo Delicata)

There was always an abundance of parcels and luggage trolleys around Waterloo back then, as almost everything went by rail, not to mention the large number always required to handle the arrival of boat trains. No such glamour for Standard 5MT No. 73084 *Tintagel* with a semi-fast service in June 1964.
(Late Norman Browne/Strathwood Library Collection)

Admiration for the footplate crew of Merchant Navy No. 35014 *Nederland Line* at Waterloo in 1964. (Late Norman Browne/Strathwood Library Collection)

Whereas solitary confinement in a 12-COR rake for Portsmouth Harbour on the penultimate day of 1966 for this motorman. (John Green)

A brief moment for a chat and a break in activity at Waterloo for three station pilots, Nos 41284, 80154 and 82029 on 30 December 1966, discussing New Year's resolutions perhaps? (John Green)

Winter sunshine again on 19 March 1961 for a chance of a run behind Adams Radial No. 30582 which will take a circuitous REC tour through the suburbs to Guildford and Leatherhead and back from Waterloo. (Robert Western)

The Nine Elms running foreman is making his rounds while Merchant Navy No. 35011 *General Steam Navigation* has just taken coal and runs back towards the turntable in 1965. (Bob Treacher/Alton Model Centre)

The fireman trims his coal for the next run in the tender of Urie S15 No. 30509 at Nine Elms in 1962. (Richard Sinclair Collection/Strathwood Library Collection)

Early spring of 1967 and the future for Nine Elms is not looking good, as seen in this view from the nearby flats on the last Easter Sunday in the steam era. (John Green)

Trouble afoot as Standard 3MT No. 82019 prepares the Nine Elms breakdown crane for duties in 1964. (Bob Treacher/Alton Model Centre)

Rudimentary, ugly, functional, powerful, distinctive, have all been used to describe Bulleid's Q1s such as No. 33020 seen here in the shed yard during 1964. Loath them or love them – which camp do you fall into? (Strathwood Library Collection)

The last day or two of steam pilots for Clapham Junction in late June 1967 find Ivatt 2MT dealing with empty stock for Waterloo and hopefully a steam-hauled departure to enjoy shortly after. (Strathwood Library Collection)

Running easy through Clapham Junction is West Country No. 34108 *Wincanton* with the 17.41 Waterloo–Salisbury, most likely right on the tail of the preceding train, on 16 May 1966. (Strathwood Library Collection)

Observing the speed restriction as well is Lord Nelson No. 30856 *Lord St Vincent* in early 1960. (Late Norman Browne/Strathwood Library Collection)

Standard 3MT No. 82029 will never be cleaned again when seen on pilot work here at Clapham Junction in June 1967. (I Lewis/Strathwood Library collection)

Eastleigh Interlude

Happily standards were much higher in 1960 when Lord Nelson No. 30863 *Lord Rodney* had pulled up for a stop at Eastleigh. This Maunsell design had been built in the works here thirty-one years previously. (Trans Pennine Publishing)

A scene seven years later suggests what it would all come to with Battle of Britain No. 34052 without the *Lord Dowding* nameplates, but at least clean, when in charge of a Basingstoke to Southampton stopper. (Derek Whitnell)

Perhaps the excuse for painting USA tanks into lined green was their use on boat trains within the Southampton Docks, rather than their use as pilots within Eastleigh Works such as here with No. 30073 on 18 April 1964. (Strathwood Library Collection)

The practice of dumping engines for both works repairs and cutting up at this location had been a long one. A very down at heel Lord Nelson No. 30864 *Sir Martin Frobisher*, seen here on 26 March 1960, would live another day or two after repairs, until January 1962. (Frank Hornby)

Returning to traffic is Maunsell King Arthur No. 30788 *Sir Urre of the Mount* on 26 March 1960, likewise another short life expectancy as she would be taken out of service in February 1962. A few days after this photograph we were singing along to Lonnie Donegan with his hit 'My Old Man's a Dustman'. (Frank Hornby)

Clearing her cylinders during the short spell that the Urie H16s were briefly tried out at Eastleigh as No. 30516 runs past on the Southampton line, also on 26 March 1960. (Frank Hornby)

Declared as withdrawn in December 1962 was Drummond's 700 Class No. 30316, set aside at Eastleigh shed fitted for snow plough duties just in case. This month was a bad one for the region's steam locomotives as the accountants authorised a large cull as witnessed in the issues of the railway magazines and society journals of the time. The cutters would be kept very busy in 1963. (Peter Simmonds)

Getting away from the station and seen from the road bridge leading to the works and sheds on a winter's morning in 1965 is Standard 5MT 73020. (Jack Hodgkinson)

Sussex and Kent Ramblings

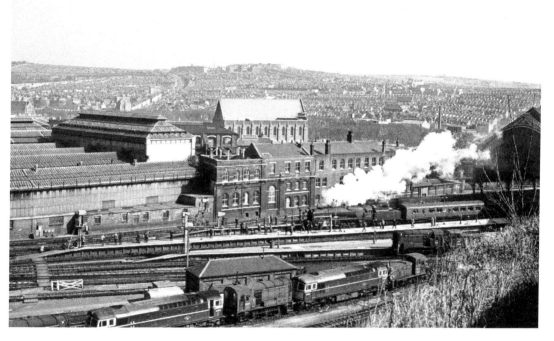

The Southern Counties Touring Society arranged Southern Rambler is standing at Brighton behind West Country No. 34108, the erstwhile *Wincanton*, on 19 March 1967. A number of spotters are on the platforms and have no doubt recorded details of the four shunters and the brace of Cromptons stabled close by. Battle of Britain No. 34056 *Croydon* had been requested, but was withdrawn the previous month. Classmate No. 34089 *602 Squadron* was the booked locomotive but a filthy No. 34108 substituted from the start. The ECS was brought into Victoria by Standard 4MT No. 80085, and returned to Clapham Yard by the same locomotive – the only other steam seen on the Central Section that day. The ECS working was notable for making a 20-mile 'round the houses' journey of over an hour because of engineering works, viz.:- Clapham Yard – Longhedge Jn – Factory Jn – Herne Hill – Tulse Hill – Crystal Palace – Norwood Junction – Selhurst – Balham – Clapham Junction – Victoria. (Strathwood Library collection)

A scorching hot day for the LCGB-organised The Sussex Coast Limited and Drummond M7 No. 30055 has plenty of spectators at Rotherfield on 24 June 1962. This would prove to be a good value tour, lasting eleven hours whilst covering 233 miles from Waterloo and back to London Bridge, utilising the preserved T9 120, Billington's K No. 32353, E6 No. 32417, E4 No. 32503 as well as this M7. (Late Vincent Heckford/Strathwood Library Collection)

Catching the eyes of passengers on the down platform at Ashford is Standard 4MT No. 80066 on 3 June 1961. No doubt playing at the town's cinema that year would be the Disney creation of *101 Dalmatians* and, for grown ups, *Breakfast at Tiffany's* starring George Peppard and Audrey Hepburn with her sunglasses and that black dress! (Frank Hornby)

A chance to record Maunsell King Arthur No. 30782 *Sir Brian* briefly at the Ramsgate stop on 25 February 1962. The tour commemorated the end of steam in Kent. Phase I of the Kent Coast electrification (Victoria–Ramsgate & Dover via Chatham plus the Sheerness branch) had been completed in June 1959 & phase II (Charing Cross to Ramsgate via Dover, Canterbury West plus Paddock Wood–Maidstone West) was due for completion in June 1962 . However, some electric trains had been running in steam timings since the previous year & any non-electric trains were worked by diesels. Hence there was virtually no steam in Kent by this time. Upon reaching Deal it was snowing heavily and the snow continued on and off for much of the day. (Trans Pennine Publishing)

More Kentish last runs with Standard 4MT 80142 at Eridge for the 18.34 Eastbourne–Tunbridge Wells West on 11 June 1965. (Strathwood Library Collection)

Built in the works of the London, Brighton and South Coast Railway in the famous seaside resort in 1900 to a design of Billington first introduced in 1897 and classified as E4, seventy had passed into British Railways ownership in 1948. At the end of 1962 a few months after this shot of No. 32503 on 27 October 1962 just four would survive and this was one. We see her employed at Kemp Town having arrived on a trip from Brighton. (Peter Simmonds)

Withdrawn a month earlier than the E4 above was Maunsell U1 No. 31891, rolling through Three Bridges on 23 March 1961. Earlier in the month one of the country's most popular entertainers, George Formby, died after suffering a heart attack. Aged 56, the Lancashire born Ukelele player was one of the UK's best-paid stars during his heyday in the 1930s and 1940s. (F G Cockman/Strathwood Library Collection)

Many branches in Kent and Sussex were to receive special treatment from the good doctor. Among the fatalities before he would even publish his famous report, *The Reshaping of British Railways*, would be the Hawkhurst branch which left the Ashford main line near Paddock Wood. Engaged on the service at Cranbrook on 13 May 1961 was Wainwright H 31308. Weeks later and it would all be over for the villages of Goudhurst and Horsmondham, also served by the branch, as closure came on 12 June 1961. (Strathwood Library Collection)

A close-up of another Wainwright H Class No. 31543 this time at Brighton in 1962. These were popular and robust engines, that were displaced as the Kent coast electrification took place. Increased numbers of Standards along with closures reduced their numbers from thirty-three examples in 1960, to fifteen in 1961 and just seven by the year's end. (Peter Simmonds)

One branch that would see off steam would be from Appledore to New Romney, closing on 6 March 1967. Our cameraman recorded a Standard 4MT at New Romney, which was convenient for visits to the Romney, Hythe and Dymchurch Railway on 4 June 1960. (Frank Hornby)

Chase the ACE

Much traffic was derived from the creamery at Seaton Junction where we find West Country No. 34107 *Blandford Forum* given the starter for the 15.15 Salisbury–Exeter Central on 22 August 1964. During the month, the United Nations had brokered another ceasefire in Cyprus, defusing the growing crisis between Greek and Turkish Cypriots and heading off the threat of invasion by Turkey. As we know with hindsight, this only lasted ten years as it kicked off again in the summer of 1974 when Turkey did invade, resulting in much bloodshed. (Strathwood Library Collection)

Back to a much more peaceful Exeter Central in 1964 with Battle of Britain No. 34081 *92 Squadron* shuffling around the station limits light engine and a standard 4MT standing in the bay behind. (Trans Pennine Publishing)

No great hurry at Salisbury during the summer of 1964 as Standard 5MT No. 73162 and Maunsell U Class No. 31798 have pulled up with the same headcodes. This was the last month or so that the Mogul would remain in service. (Trans Pennine Publishing)

Double-heading for the heavier summer holiday through trains from Waterloo to Axminster for the run along the almost seven miles to Lyme Regis here in 1960. (Phil Nunn Collection)

Ivatt 2MT No. 41216 draws a goods including china-clay wagons into Torrington during 1963. (Trans Pennine Publishing)

More Ivatt tanks congregate within the rather shabby engine shed at Barnstaple months before closure in 1964. (Trans Pennine Publishing)

Trains were divided and combined at Exeter Central where we see No. 34075 *264 Squadron* the previous year. (Trans Pennine Publishing)

Active in shunting near Exmouth Junction shed was Maunsell Z Class No. 30951 on 20 July 1962. Strathwood (Library Collection)

It must have been a warm day on 11 June 1967 for this party picnicking whilst waiting for the passing of West Country No. 34023 *Blackmore Vale* near Salisbury working its leg of the Warwickshire Railway Society's Farewell to LSWR Steam Tour. (Strathwood Library Collection)

Another Farewell to Steam Tour, this time from the Southern Counties Touring Society, brought Riddles 9F No. 92220 *Evening Star* to Seaton Junction on 20 September 1964. (Strathwood Library Collection)

Western Region incursion to Barnstaple Junction with a Taunton train behind Churchward Mogul No. 7304 on 22 June 1963. (Peter Simmonds)

Heading west would be almost everything from Salisbury's yard for cutting in Welsh scrapyards by July 1967. However a reprieve would come for this engine and it would head back to Eastleigh in January 1968 before preservation. (Strathwood Library Collection)

Signs of Western Region DMUs being sheltered in the sheds at Salisbury bode badly for twelve-year-old Standard 5MT No. 73093 at Salisbury on 4 June 1967. (Strathwood Library Collection)

Displaced from work around London by November 1962 was Maunsell W No. 31914, seen at Exeter Central in 1963 whilst based at Exmouth Junction. By December 1963 it would make its way back along the LSWR main line to spend its last eight months back closer to London, based on 70B Feltham. (Trans Pennine Publishing)

Islanders Part One

The view from the parallel road bridge towards Terrier No. 32678 making one of the many then daily runs across the Langston Bridge on 26 August 1962. (Frank Hornby)

It was of course the limitations of weight on this bridge that allowed the survival of these little o-6-os, which would also be a blessing for the Bluebell Railways in preservation. With the spark arrester standing proud on her chimney is No. 32646, on a Down train again at Langston Bridge on 14 September 1963. (Peter Simmonds)

The engine's profile against the unique glass-fibre-bodied British Railways coach is evident on No. 32650 as she awaits departure at Havant on 15 June 1963. (Peter Simmonds)

Running around on arrival at Hayling Island during 1963 for the 1872-built No. 32670 which had been sold out of service to the Kent & East Sussex Railway becoming their number 3, before being bought back again forty-seven years later for duties such as this. Upon closure of the line she would find a new life in preservation. (Late Vincent Heckford/Strathwood Library Collection)

The branch ran its last passenger train on 4 November 1963, just as Gerry and the Pacemakers were riding high in the charts with 'You'll Never Walk Alone'. A few weeks before, on 14 September 1963, an Up train, No. 32646 comes off the bridge with an Up train at Langston. (Peter Simmonds)

Just arrived at Hayling Island from Havant on 26 August 1962 was another of the class, No. 32661, which had been numbered 61 and awarded the name *Sutton* when new in 1975. (Frank Hornby)

Retreating up into the head shunt at Havant to run round its coaches during 1 June 1963 was No. 32678, which also had an interesting career, being withdrawn in 1925. Four years later it was put through works and sent to the Isle of Wight, eventually becoming W14 *Bembridge*, returning to the mainland as No. 2678 once more in 1946. Determined to survive this is another Terrier to pass into preservation. (Simmonds)

The day before the end on the branch, 3 November 1963, saw the LCGB run their Hayling Island Farewell Tour which brought Battle of Britain No. 34088 *213 Squadron* to work the short leg from Fratton to Portsmouth. (Strathwood Library Collection)

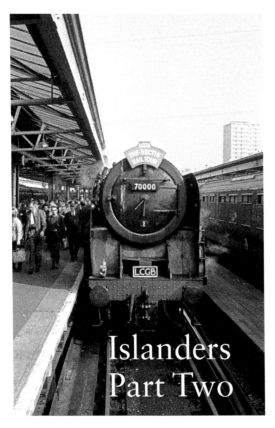

Islanders Part Two

Left: Alighting from another LCGB special at Portsmouth Harbour on 4 October the following year, which had enjoyed a run from Guildford via Reading General, Basingstoke, Eastleigh, and Fareham to arrive here, which can be best described as the Cook's tour behind *Britannia* herself. (Strathwood Library Collection)

Below: Joining one of the paddle steamers for our passage across the Solent to arrive at Ryde, this time on 1 June 1963. (Peter Simmonds)

Stopped just short of the buffers at Ryde Pier Head is Adams O2 W22 *Brading* on a balmy Sunday 28 August 1966. (Peter Coton)

The footplate crew are relaxed on board W29 *Alverstone* as they await departure from Ryde Pier head on 31 August the previous year. (Strathwood Library Collection)

Another view of W29 *Alverstone* coming off the pier again in 1965 with another load of passengers off a paddle steamer moored in the background. (Richard Sinclair Collection/Strathwood Library Collection)

Getting away from Ryde St Johns Road on an August bank holiday weekend in 1965 is W22 *Brading*, allowing us the chance to get around the engine shed here. (Dave Down)

With seven O2s on shed, this cannot be a bank holiday weekend at Ryde St Johns, although it is 1965. The shed coded 70H did not close to steam until March 1967, as it seems several locos were used after the end in December 1966 for track-lifting trains. (Strathwood Library Collection)

Footplate work was clearly warm on 1 June 1963 for this chap on board W35 *Freshwater*, pulling away from Brading. The newspapers were full of a more serious scandal at the time. Secretary of State for War John Profumo would resign from government, admitting he lied to Parliament about his relationship with a call girl. Prime Minister Harold Macmillan accepted the resignation, calling it a 'great tragedy'. John Profumo, 48, made a personal statement to the House of Commons on 22 March in which he admitted being misleading about his relationship with 21-year-old call girl Christine Keeler. (Peter Simmonds)

A passing moment at Brading on 9 July 1966. W17 *Seaview* arrives with the 11.10 SO Ryde Pier head–Shanklin as W24 *Calbourne*, now reduced to unlined black livery, will leave with the 11.14 SO Shanklin–Ryde Pier head. (Stewart Blencowe Collection)

An overtaking manoeuvre at Sandown with W29 *Alverstone* on the 08.40 Ventnor–Ryde passing W20 *Shanklin* in the loop on 7 August 1966. Young boys all across England would be playing football in the streets and parks pretending to be the stars who had just won the World Cup a week before. (Strathwood Library Collection)

Staff observe the passing of two trains again, this time at Wroxall with W33 *Bembridge* nearest the camera on a Ventnor train on 1 June 1966. (Peter Simmonds)

Trundling along between Wroxall and Shanklin is W30 *Shorwell* on 1 June 1963, this locomotive was taken out of service in September 1965 and remained stored on the island to become the last of her class, cut up as late as November 1967. (Peter Simmonds)

A heartwarming scene of a father and son taking in the details of W26 *Whitwell* as it awaits departure from Ventnor on 3 August 1965. Keeping many youngsters hooked to the television in 1965 was Gerry Anderson's *Thunderbirds*, with all the spin-off associated toys even then. (Dave Down)

This young fireman tends to the needs of his engine, W20 *Shanklin*, at Ventnor under the eyes of waiting passengers. Hence it seems he has the water turned on slowly, not wishing to soak himself under their gaze, on 1 September 1965. (Dave Down)

A mother gives her child a better view of W17 *Seaview* leaving bunker-first from Haven Street with the 09.31 Cowes–Ryde past the well-kept gardens on 4 June 1963. (Strathwood Library Collection)

Taking the waters again, this time at Newport on W18 *Ningwood* in 1963. Not much need for the fire devil to prevent frost problems just yet. (Trans Pennine Publishing)

About to conduct the run round arrangement at Cowes during 1963 is W14 *Fishbourne*, allowing the coaches to roll back under control of the guard and his brake, thus freeing the incoming locomotive. (Trans Pennine Publishing)

Having checked all is well this footplate man returns to W27 *Merstone* for the departure from Cowes back to Ryde on 1 June 1963. (Peter Simmonds)

As W28 *Ashey* runs along Ryde Pier on 31 August 1965, we will take our leave of the Isle of Wight via a hovercraft bound for Southampton. (Dave Down)

Around
Southampton

The double pegs are clear for West Country No. 34001 *Exeter* at Southampton Central in 1964, but the driver will not be hurried as he has an oil round before departure. (Trans Pennine Publishing)

Sweeping around the curve at Northam and away from the line to the terminus was West Country No. 34101 *Hartland* on 3 June 1965 with a Down Bournemouth train. (Strathwood Library Collection)

Beyond the Terminus station and into the docks, USA No. 30071 makes full use of its short wheel base around the many tight curves within this vast complex of lines serving both goods and passengers on 19 June 1965. (Stewart Blencowe Collection)

Introduced to replace the USA tanks and E2s from 1962 were these Ruston & Hornsby 0-6-0 diesel shunters, with this one pushing a horsebox into one of the sheds on 19 June 1965. (Stewart Blencowe Collection)

Filthy dirty but at least wearing nameplates in 1967 is West Country No. 34018 *Axminster* heading for Bournemouth. The third rails are already in place for electric services when ready. (Michael Beaton)

The Down Bournemouth Belle comes past Millbrook station on 4 June 1966 with West Country No. 34026 *Yes Tor* in charge. Such was the prowess of Eastleigh Works in the rebuilding programme for the Bulleid Pacifics that *Yes Tor* was dealt with in just five weeks from 9 January 1958 and was released again on 15 February 1958. (Strathwood Library Collection)

No cleaners around to look after No. 35021 *New Zealand Line*, it seems, as she pulls up in Southampton Central during 1963. (Trans Pennine Publishing)

On 19 March 1966 the LCGB ran their New Forester Rail Tour which utilised USA tanks Nos 30073/63 along the branch to Fawley seen at the top and then along the branch where it was much photographed, it seems. (All three photographs from the Strathwood Library Collection)

Here we see some Bulleid contrasts at Southampton Central. Firstly with Battle of Britain No. 34050 *Royal Observer Corps* running light engine through the station in 1963. (Late Ray Helm)

Contrasting badly with the modernising railways image which presented steam as filthy, leaky and probably unreliable as in this image of Merchant Navy No. 35007 *Port Line* as the construction cranes go up for the rebuilding of the Southampton Central station area in late 1966. (Strathwood Library Collection)

Standard 5MT No. 73029, which is actually lined green under the muck, brings a clean rake of Bulleid coaches into Millbrook with a Bournemouth stopping train on 8 October 1966. (Michael Beaton)

Seen on the same day was Battle of Britain No. 34089 *602 Squadron* at a state of readiness in Southampton Central to go towards Bournemouth. (Michael Beaton)

Specials

A chat with the footplate crew of Riddles 9F No. 92220 *Evening Star* before departure from Victoria on 20 September 1964. This is the start of the SCTS special we saw at Seaton Junction on page 29. As was usual with so many tours, it was booked via a very stretched route which, in this case, would have brought the locomotive back via East Putney. However, it was diverted via Chertsey and Twickenham as it was discovered at a late stage that the loco's ATC ramp would have fouled the fourth rail for the London Transport District Line on East Putney route. (Strathwood Library Collection)

Once again a last minute exchange with the driver of the now preserved Gresley K4 No. 3442 *The Great Marquess* within the overall roof of London's Victoria station on 12 March 1967. All did not go to plan that day, as owing to a track circuit failure the tour terminated at Preston Park, the 19.05 Littlehampton–Victoria service train making a special stop to pick up the tour passengers to get them back to London. (Strathwood Library Collection)

Such was the demand for a final run behind the two Beattie Well Tanks Nos 30587 and 30585 that two identical tours were run; one on 2 December and this one seen at Hampton Court on 16 December 1962. Immediately after the second tour the three remaining Beattie 2-4-0WTs were withdrawn. (Strathwood Library Collection)

A jointly arranged RCTS/LCGB special has stopped for photographers at Frimley behind Maunsell S15 No. 30839 in third-rail territory at Frimley on 18 October 1965. (Strathwood Library Collection)

The weather has not been so kind to photographers using slow films on 26 March 1966 with Gresley A4 No. 60024 *Kingfisher* being serviced at Eastleigh. (Derek Whitnell)

Although it was that scorching day described with M7 No. 30055 on page 20, tweed jackets and pullovers are in evidence while Billington K Class No. 32353 stands in platform 3 at Portsmouth Harbour station. (Late Vincent Heckford/Strathwood Library Collection)

The same tour on 24 June 1962 and with an 11-minute stop booked at Cranleigh, another chance to get out and stretch the legs and grab another photograph, this time with Drummond T9 No. 120 as she waits to take the train another 11 miles to the first engine change at Horsham. (Late Vincent Heckford/Strathwood Library Collection)

A Maunsell U and N Class Mogul combination of Nos 31803 and 31411 near Heathfield on 13 June 1965 with
The Wealdsman Rail Tour run by the LCGB. (Strathwood Library Collection)

Devoid of nameplates, Battle of Britain No. 34052 *Lord Dowding* was one of four engines used on the SCTS Four Counties tour of 9 October 1966 passing Shalford Junction. The others being No. 35023 *Holland-Afrika Line*, No. 80154 and No. 30072. (Strathwood Library Collection)

Getting a run from Victoria to Eastleigh via Brighton and return behind Gresley A3 No. 4472 *Flying Scotsman*, seen here at Eastleigh preparing for the run back to London and at this point facing south on 17 September 1966. (Strathwood Library Collection)

Another interloper, this time from Scotland, for the LCGB A2 Commemorative Railtour was No. 60532 *Blue Peter*, with drain cocks open and not running well, it has to be said, near Clapham Junction on 14 August 1966. The Peppercorn Pacific stopped on Honiton bank short of steam and, after arrival at Exeter Central, retired to Exmouth Junction for some attention. It had been intended that the A2 would take over again at Salisbury but Britannia No. 70004 *William Shakespeare* ran through to Waterloo to recover some of the lost time. (Strathwood Library Collection)

Not all rail tours were marathon events involving many locomotives. The Plymouth Railway Circle ran The Wenford Special from Wadebridge to Wenford Bridge and back on 19 September 1964, using 1366 Class Pannier Tank No. 1369 and a mixed rake of brake vans. (Dave Down)

A pairing of Maunsell U No. 31639 and Standard 4MT No. 75070 draws into Fareham as part of The Solent Rail Tour run by the RCTS on 20 March 1966. (Strathwood Library Collection)

The first of two specials in January 1966 to commemorate the end of the S15s was in sunshine on the 9th as No. 30837 climbs past Medstead, whereas the second run on the 16th ran in snow over this section of what is known as the Alps. (Strathwood Library Collection)

The keen-eyed will notice that the Feltham-based S15 has also been bulled up with painted buffers and smoke box straps for this second run, paused at Alton on 16 January 1966. Beside it being World Cup year, it was also the start of that great alternative sporting event, *It's a Knockout*. The joy of the television coverage was amplified a thousand times when local Manchester newsreader Stuart Hall got his hands on it. Stuart had the ability to laugh for hours on end at the drop of a hat (or bucket of bright yellow water). Once he was paired with the almost indecipherable rugby commentator Eddie Waring, it was possible to get through whole shows without a single complete sentence being uttered. (Strathwood Library Collection)

That Maunsell mogul pairing of Nos 31803 and 31411 seen on page 57 has stopped at Heathfield, allowing the opportunity to explore the station limits on 13 June 1965. (Strathwood Library Collection)

Reading
to Redhill

The confidently relaxed glance back along his train and to our cameraman is from a senior driver in charge of Maunsell N Mogul No. 31862 at Reading in 1964. (Trans Pennine Publishing)

Another of the Moguls, nicknamed U Boats from Maunsell's U Class No. 31799, has a clear run signalled ahead at Farnborough North while working a Reading–Redhill service again in 1964. (Strathwood Library Collection)

The route passed underneath the LSWR main line near Ash Vale, where we see the passing of the Bournemouth Belle behind West Country No. 34008 *Padstow* in April 1966.
(Late Norman Browne/Strathwood Library Collection)

About to make the stop for North Camp with the 14.50 Reading–Redhill service on 26 September 1964 is one of the stalwarts of the route, Maunsell N No. 31831. The 1964/65 football season was underway, which would end in a thrilling climax between Leeds United and Manchester United, and would favour the latter team on goal difference as they both finished on 61 points. (Strathwood Library Collection)

A chilly morning in 1964 as the rosebay willowherb, or fireweed, goes over. One of Churchward's Moguls, No. 7327, gets a run on the route, which would often see even a Manor filling in on a Reading–Redhill service. (Late Norman Browne/Strathwood Library Collection)

A return to the usual diet of Maunsell Moguls in the shape of N Class No. 31405 arriving at North Camp with the 13.16 Ash–Reading train on 12 September 1964. Three days later *The Sun* newspaper is published for the first time. It replaced the Mirror Group's *Daily Herald*, which had been losing readers and advertising revenue for several years. This new arrival on Fleet Street promised to follow a radical and independent agenda – unlike its predecessor, which had strong ties to the Labour party, the TUC having sold its 49 per cent stake in the paper in 1960. (Strathwood Library Collection)

The double-chimney-fitted Standard 4MT No. 75076 keeps company with Battle of Britain No. 34049 *Anti-Aircraft Command* with its distinctive red-backed badge as they await their next turns from Guildford around 1962. (Trans Pennine Publishing)

The need for a short wheel base locomotive to move dead engines from road to road around the round shed layout accessed via the turntable at Guildford kept Adams B4 No. 30089 employed in the early sixties. (Trans Pennine Publishing)

One of Maunsell's Q Class 0-6-0s No. 30543 on the turntable at Guildford in August 1964. Listed as withdrawn that December it went along with No. 30530 to be broken up at Ward's of Grays in Essex in May 1965. (Late Norman Browne/Strathwood Library Collection)

A sunny morning at Reigate welcomes Standard 4MT No. 80152 working the 09.03 Reading–Redhill service on 27 September 1964. (Strathwood Library Collection)

Enthusiasts armed with cameras are out to record the last steam workings in the winter sun as Standard 4MT No. 80089 remains at Redhill for the 15.13 to Tonbridge as our steam-hauled train departs on 2 January 1965. (Strathwood Library Collection)

Just put on to the LCGB Maunsell Commemorative Rail Tour in Redhill Yard is N Class No. 31411 on 3 January 1965, having replaced classmate No. 31831 off the leg from Reading Southern. (Strathwood Library Collection)

Hants and Dorset Byways

The Great Western Railway had a station right in Southern territory at Winchester Chesil which saw little traffic, as demonstrated in this view of one of the then-new DEMUs No. 1112, calling here just before the closure to passengers in 1960. (Strathwood Library Collection)

No mistaking where we are now from the running-in board, although as all trains had to stop here before running into the Solent, was it really overkill as we catch Drummond M7 No. 30254 backing empty coaching stock back out on 31 May 1963. In the charts, The Beatles blocked the number one spot for seven weeks with 'From Me to You'. (Strathwood Library Collection)

Crossing the empty stock for another service pulled by a fellow M7 is No. 30129 at Lymington Town with the 10.18 to the pier on 1 June 1963. (Strathward Library Collection)

The 07.20 train from Lymington pies to Brockenhurst departs under the watchful eye of the footplate crew on 1 May 1963. (Strathward Library Collection)

On 25 March 1967 the Manchester Rail Travel Society ran their Hants & Dorset Branch Flyer which employed Standard 4MT No. 80151 along the 5 ¼ mile branch from Brockenhurst. The gallery has assembled for the chance to record the running round of the train at Lymington Pier. (Peter Simmonds)

The signal is being given to the driver of another of the class, No. 80011 at Lymington Pier on 3 March 1967. No room for overrunning the buffer stops without an awful lot of explaining to do. (Strathwood Library Collection)

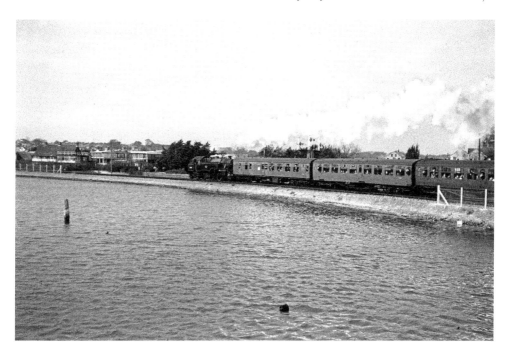

Above: Departing back up the branch with its tour train once more is Standard 4MT No. 80151 and away from Lymington Pier on 25 March 1967. (Peter Simmonds)

Right: At Brockenhurst the locomotive takes water at the platform where the anxious station master points a stern finger to our cameraman, perhaps about the newly laid third rail being live for testing. (Strathwood Library Collection)

Just a two-coach load for Standard 4MT 76010 at Blue Pool Bridge with the 16.03 Swanage–Wareham on 4 September 1966. (Strathwood Library Collection)

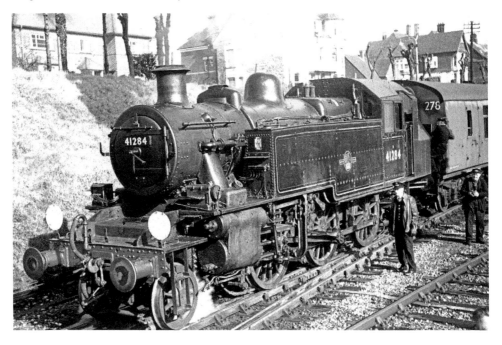

The first of two Ivatt 2MTs, No. 41284, couples up for the return special at Swanage to await No. 41301 which will act as pilot on Sunday 27 February 1966 back to the main-line connection at Wareham. (Peter Coton)

One of the Ivatts, No. 41284 is seen once more at Easton on a special on 27 March 1965. Advertised locally by the South & West Railway Society there were three round trips – Saturday morning, lunchtime & afternoon from Melcombe Regis (Weymouth) through Portland to Easton. (Strathwood Library Collection)

An earlier special traversed the branch to Easton, which closed to passengers in 1952, behind 57xx Pannier No. 3737 on 14 August 1960 as part of the RCTS Greyhound tour, which also used T9 No. 30718 and L Class No. 31768 that day. (Strathwood Library Collection)

Even working as far as Waterloo one evening, the borrowed Black Five No. 45493 was found making good progress through Parkstone with the 10.30 Poole–York on 30 May 1966. (Strathwood Library Collection)

In an attempt to smarten up the appearance of the Bournemouth Belle to the public, Western Region chocolate-and-cream-liveried full brakes were used to try and match the burnt-umber-and-cream liveries of the Pullman cars to afford the extra luggage capacity required on the train, instead of the native green ones, although even blue-and-grey ones turned up in the end. Looking at the state of Merchant Navy No. 35003 *Royal Mail*, one wonders why they could not clean the rostered locomotive for this working in 1966, unless Royal Mail was standing in for a failure. Either way it was a pity that standards had fallen this low. (Strathwood Library Collection)

Joining a party of spotters visiting the shed at Bournemouth on 8 March 1964 where Standard 4MT No. 76015 parked up outside in the yard. (Winston Cole)

The declining standards of locomotive care are all too evident again on West Country No. 34034 *Honiton* which has called at Pokesdown with a Saturday extra from the north on 20 August 1966. (John Sansom)

Accelerating away from Bournemouth on 9 September 1965 was Battle of Britain No. 34053 *Sir Keith Park*. Making us laugh at the cinema in 1965 were the *Carry On* team led by Sid James as the Rumpo Kid, terrorising Stodge City in *Carry On Cowboy*. (Jack Hodgkinson)

Sweeping past exactly one year later going to the shed at Bournemouth was Standard 5MT No. 73002 on 9 September 1966. (John Sansom)

A busy moment at Bournemouth Central in 1962, with West Country No. 34024 *Tamar Valley* alongside Battle of Britain No. 34090 *Sir Eustace Missenden*, Southern Railway. Lurking in the shadows of the roof is a Standard on another through road. (Trans Pennine Publishing)

The track work around the station would be changed radically in the electric era, to accommodate the new traction. Although Standard 4MT No. 75076 is seen standing on the shed at Bournemouth on 4 March 1967, the platforms for the carriage cleaner are in place in preparation for the REP, VEP and TC stock soon to take over. (John Sansom)

Stopping off at Basingstoke

Approaching from the south-west on 24 July 1965 was Merchant Navy No. 35011 *General Steam Navigation*. Taken out of traffic in February 1966 the engine would linger at Eastleigh until March just over a year later before being dragged to Barry, in theory for scrapping. (Michael Beaton)

Much photographed by many cameramen it seems was Maunsell U Class No. 31639 making its way past the shed towards the station in October 1965. (Strathwood Library Collection)

Less photographed in colour was Maunsell Schools No. 30919 *Harrow*, although many a lad most likely made up the Airfix plastic kit with artwork depicting this one in the sixties. (Trans Pennine Publishing)

Bringing a tell-tale train for the London Midland Region into Basingstoke in September 1964 is West Country No. 34047 *Callington* which will take the Basingstoke route towards Reading, Didcot and most likely change engines at Oxford. (Strathwood Library Collection)

Passing through the town in August 1963 is Merchant Navy No. 35026 *Lamport & Holt Line* which was one of the last batch of ten of the class completed after nationalisation in 1948. One wonders today if the railways had not been taken into government ownership, would there have been any more batches built in their original form? (Strathwood Library Collection)

Bringing a little extra glamour perhaps to Basingstoke shed was *Flying Scotsman*, seen in the background as West Country No. 34047 *Callington* comes through with an express on 12 September 1964. (Strathwood Library Collection)

Signalled away from Basingstoke is Maunsell N No. 31858 in 1964, one of thirty of the eighty-strong class built at Ashford Works in 1925, with the last fifteen being turned out between 1932 and 1934. (Strathwood Library Collection)

Construction of the forty members of the class of Q1s was also split but between both Ashford and Brighton, with all of them going into service between March and December 1942. One of the Ashford-built, No. 33027, heads for Eastleigh with a goods on 7 August 1965. (Michael Beaton)

Running fast towards Worting Junction and the Salisbury route is Merchant Navy No. 35001 *Channel Packet* with the Down Atlantic Coast Express in August 1963. (Strathwood Library Collection)

A more leisurely timing is afforded to Battle of Britain No. 34066 *Spitfire* with her train on Sunday 10 April 1966 to allow water to be taken from the Down platform. (Peter Coton)

Consecutive-numbered West Countries No. 34093 *Saunton* and No. 34092 *City of Wells* side by side allow comparison of the rebuild against the original's air smoothed design. (John Newman)

The smoke deflectors fitted as part of the rebuild to Battle of Britain No. 34052 *Lord Dowding* are clearly little use at slow speeds such as here in September 1963. (Stuart R. Harris)

Coming from the Western Region via Reading West, one of Churchward's 2800 Class No. 2856 from 81C Southall approaches Worting Junction in August 1963. (Strathwood Library Collection)

Picking up speed at Worting Junction is West Country 34017 Ilfracombe in July of 1966. During this summer, England were enjoying less success on the cricket pitches as Gary Sobers was in superb form for the West Indies, helping them to a 3-1 defeat of England with one match drawn. (Jerry Beddows)

Getting down trackside at the same location for Standard 5MT No. 73155 running fast past the freshly laid third rail. (Jerry Beddows)

Along with the electric services would come new signalling, making Worting Junction signal box redundant as it would all be controlled from Basingstoke. Meanwhile West Country No. 34002 *Salisbury* comes off the Eastleigh lines on with an Up passenger working on 20 May 1966. (Jerry Beddows)

Early Preservation Roots

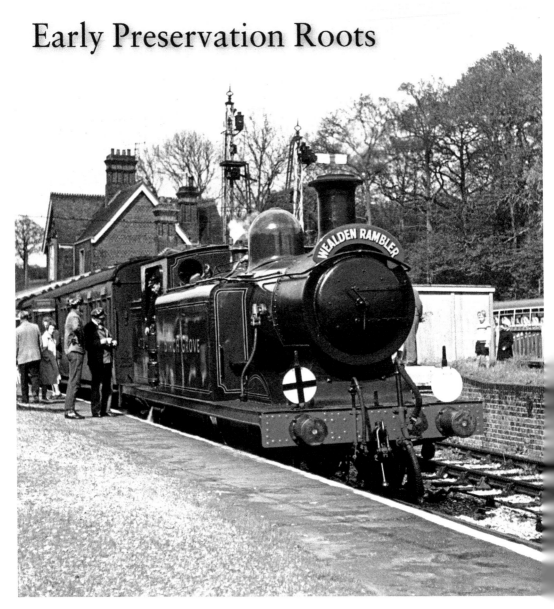

Less than six months from being withdrawn by British Railways, Billington E4 No. 32473 is back in steam again painted into its London Brighton & South Coast Railway identity as *Birch Grove*, being admired by two youngsters on the opposite platform at Sheffield Park on 11 May 1963.

The groundwork for this had begun in Spring 1959 with the formation of the Lewes & East Grinstead Railway Preservation Society, the forerunner of today's Bluebell Railway Preservation Society. In the early days the initial aim was to re-open the whole line from East Grinstead to Culver Junction, and to run it as a commercial service. This was envisaged as using a diesel railcar, as soon as funds allowed. These plans sadly came to nothing, for two reasons. Firstly, the society failed to purchase the whole line and secondly, most local residents were not that interested. So in the interim, the re-opening of the section of line from Sheffield Park to Bluebell Halt just south of Horsted Keynes (which was at first leased and eventually purchased from British Railways) as both a steam railway and museum was planned and approved. (Strathwood Library Collection)

Withdrawn from Western Region running in October 1960 as No. 9017, this rather fortunate Dukedog was purchased and had found a home on the Bluebell Railway, by the time it was photographed approaching Horsted Keynes on 4 July 1965 taking on the identity as No. 3217 *Earl of Berkeley*. (Aldo Delicata)

Among the early arrivals at the blossoming Bluebell Railway was this Wainwright P Class, which had been taken out of service as No. 31323 in July 1960. Given a repaint by 10 September 1961, she was coupled to the ex-Chesham set and ready for passengers at Sheffield Park. (Frank Hornby)

A pleasant ride in the fresh air is afforded for a smoke on the footplate of Terrier No. 32636 now also in a former LB&SC guise as 72 Fenchurch departing Horsted Keynes on 22 June 1969. (Aldo Delicata)

Assuming its pre-grouping livery as well at Sheffield Park on 15 June 1963 was the former No. 30583, withdrawn in July 1961 from British Railways. (Strathwood Library Collection)

The Longmoor Military Railway was a brief host to the preservation movement, but on 16 April 1966 it was still giving active railway training to the army, as well as running specials such as here behind No. 195, an Austerity 0-6-0ST. (Winston Cole)

Sanctuary was afforded to a number of locomotives at Longmoor in the sixties including Nos 35028, 34023, 92203, 41298 and Standard 4MT No. 75029, resplendent here in the summer of 1969.
(Late Norman Browne/Strathwood Library Collection)

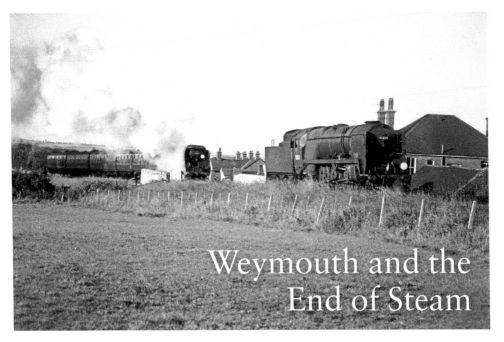

Weymouth and the End of Steam

Climbing out of Weymouth at Upwey is West Country No. 34102 *Lapford* as Merchant Navy No. 35023 *Holland-Afrika Line* drops down Upwey Bank light engine in 1967. (Late Alan Marriott/Strathwood Library Collection)

On banking duty at Weymouth on 26 March 1966 was Standard 5MT No. 73114 *Etarre*, moving into position for the shove to just beyond Bincombe Tunnel. (John Sansom)

Another visitor to the footbridge close to the engine shed at Weymouth recorded another Standard 5MT No. 73016 along with Hymek D7022 in the background in 1966. (Dennis Feltham)

Plenty of stored and never to be used again locomotives cast aside at Weymouth in the summer of 1967. The day of closure would be 9 July that year, having been a Western Region shed until 1 February 1958 when it passed to the Southern as 71G, finally at closure coded 70G. (Strathwood Library Collection)

Two years before the release of *The Italian Job* a trendy Mini Cooper is on the quayside at Weymouth Harbour as D2043 makes its walking pace journey back to the main line station in 1967. (Strathwood Library Collection)

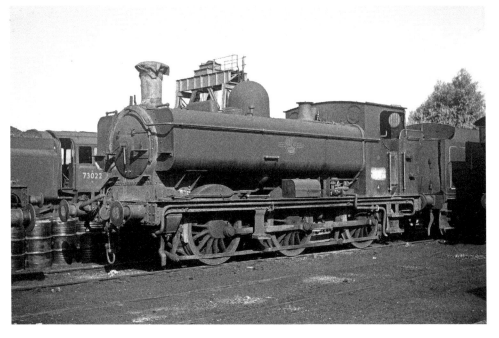

There had been plenty of work for ex-Great Western Railway pannier tanks such as No. 7780 handling the large amount of Channel Islands produce landed through the quaysides of Weymouth. However, by 18 August 1963 this one was set aside and ready for the scrap-dealers to make their bids. (Strathwood Library Collection)

Another special that went wrong was the LCGB Green Arrow Rail Tour, which brought down Gresley V2 No. 60919 from Dundee, only for the star engine to fail before even coming on the train. In the event among the engines used on 3 July 1966 were Black Five No. 45493 and West Country No. 34002 *Salisbury*, here ready to make a start for the return to London, while a Hymek with a train for the Bristol line also awaits the off. (Strathwood Library Collection)

A DMU is covering the Western Region stopping service from Weymouth in July 1962, while Standard 4MT No. 76018 sets off in July 1962. (B Griffiths/Strathwood Library Collection)

British Rail ran this official tour as a Farewell to Steam on 2 July 1967, double-headed by Merchant Navies No. 35007 *Aberdeen Commonwealth* and No. 35008 *Orient Line* disappearing into the tunnel at Upwey Wishing Well Halt. (Late Alan Marriott/Strathwood Library Collection)

Right at the end and still being used as a banker out of Weymouth and past Upwey was West Country No. 34093, now deprived of its *Saunton* nameplates. (Late Alan Marriott/Strathwood Library Collection)

Not quite what it seems but it was the last Channel Islands Boat train, which ran the day before behind Merchant Navy No. 35023 *Holland-Afrika Line* and has come down on 9 July 1967 the last day of steam as the 08.30 ex-Waterloo. (Strathwood Library Collection)

With only No. 35028 *Clan Line* expected to survive into preservation after 2 July 1967, the double-headed assault by Merchant Navies No. 35007 *Aberdeen Commonwealth* and No. 35008, *Orient Line* was thought at the time to be the very last time a pair would work in harness together on British Railways when seen making short work of Upwey Bank. (Late Alan Marriott/Strathwood Library Collection)